I0149112

All Scripture references taken from the KJV, unless otherwise indicated.

Lord, Help My Debt is book 2 of a 4-book series, *Don't Refuse Me, Lord.*

Don't Refuse Me, Lord (Book 1)

Lord, Help My Debt (Book 2)

As My Soul Prospers (Book 3)

Do Not Work for Money (Book 4)

ISBN # 978-1-893555-78-5

Paperback Version

Copyright 2022, Dr. Marlene Miles

Table of Contents

Lord, Help My Debt

Freshwater

Freshwater Press, USA

Lord, Help My Debt

Bring the money into the storehouse
so that there may be meat in mine house.
Malachi 3:11

Debt is a curse.

Many Christians cannot bring *meat* level offerings into the House of God because they are under the curse of debt and worldly financial obligations. Much debt is incurred before Salvation. The spirit is regenerated at Salvation, the soul is saved from hell, but financially, credit cards are still due in the natural, they have to be paid off by the now-saved man.

Debt is the result of sin, so spiritually, there is a sin-debt that can remain as well. God can redeem these debts all at once, or it can take time to overcome, payoff, or retire them.

Here, we are talking about two different kinds of debt: sin debt and financial debt.

The regenerated man should not be living for his flesh; he is no longer flesh-driven or flesh-led. His need for worldly items should not be as great as the urges of an unregenerated man. Even if he has old debt, prayerfully he's not creating any new debt.

I'm not saying to live in poverty, neither that the saved should have inferior goods, just that the saved man shouldn't want or buy everything he sees. So, if financial debt was a problem before, once saved, certain bondages and cycles should be broken. Through God, debt deliverance can be sudden, or there might be progressive deliverance through resisting the devil. A *spirit of greed* or *dissatisfaction* for instance could simply go dormant, or hide, only to rear its head at another inconvenient time. Still, I believe that not having a desire for something over a long term proves deliverance.

A man gets saved, but sin debt, called *iniquity* is still there. The spirit is regenerated, and the soul is saved from hell, but the acts of the flesh committed against God and the repercussions of those sins have to be dealt with. *Iniquity* means guilt worthy of punishment. Even a saved man can continue sinning (not the expectation) but it happens. Until deliverance from sin, sin can be lord over a man rather than Our God, (Romans 6:14).

When sin gets "in the blood", there must be deliverance. Sin in a family's bloodline may make a person feel compelled to sin. You may not even *want* to sin, but you just do. Perhaps in your family everyone steals. You don't want to steal, but you find yourself taking things from stores or from people's houses. *Iniquity* is causing you to have sticky fingers. It's not an excuse because you are still responsible for the sin, but it was not your intention to steal. Because of stealing, you have **debt--**, civil or natural debt, yes because you owe for what you stole. But there is also *spiritual debt* for having sinned. The natural debt is that you owe the person the thing you stole from them or the value of the thing you stole from them. Restitution is owed to them.

This gets complicated; the *spiritual punishment* of the sin may be the cause of **more** **debt** and also <u>**financial losses**</u> in the natural. The *entities* who **enforce the curse** that was created by the sin (stealing) now have an open door to steal from <u>*you*</u>. How can invisible "entities" steal from you? Any number of ways, such as: Imagined sicknesses that require medical and pharmaceutical attention. Unpaid time off from work. The car or washing machine breaks, mysteriously. Your cherished pet gets sick. Common money drains are many times a result of you owing a *spiritual debt* and this is how evil spirits collect it from you, by putting holes in your pocket. This debt may not have been caused by anything you did, it could be ancestral, evil inheritance.

Now you have less money, less everything and *more* debt. This curse from stealing, in our example, could have been in your family for generations and by stealing even once, you <u>*renew*</u> the evil covenant and the curse for *at least* another three or four generations into your bloodline. It's a never-ending process unless there is **deliverance**.

Man gets in debt trouble because of his flesh. The flesh is so *now*; it wants to be ministered to, attended to right now. Like babies, many people cannot endure even the slightest discomfort. For instance, how long can you ignore an itch before you scratch it, even in public? An eyelash in the eye--, how long before you go eyelash hunting? A temptation to do something that's in your bloodline seems nearly irresistible. You want to do that thing, now, or as soon as you can. It's like scratching an itch.

From birth, with good parents, we are loved and made very comfortable. We've been catered to as if we were guests since we were brought home from the hospital. Parents think that if they do everything perfectly for their newborn that the child will be perfect and live a perfect life, never giving a thought to the fact that **each parent** has *generational stuff* that will show up in and be walked out by their child. It's not just what the kid will look like, it's deeper than whose nose, what complexion and hair their wished-for, prayed-for "perfect" child will inherit. **In this sense hands of long-gone relatives still *touch* all of us. The actions of their lives live on to affect ours.**

Many times, it is not until the young child or teenager begins to behave badly that the "perfect child" spell cast over its parents is broken. It is not until *wa—a---ay* after infancy that parents may come to their senses and stop spoiling their child or look deeper spiritually as to why Junior is behaving *like that.*

It's them; it's their parents. It's *their* ancestors.

Sadly, sometimes the spell is never broken. The spell makes parents go overboard doing **NATURAL** things for a child, not giving a thought to the child's spiritual needs. So even though this child has *things and stuff*, the child has inherited **DEBT**. It may not be noticeable while the parents are alive to get the kid out of every pickle he/she may get into. But when left alone, spiritual debt will be evident, sooner or later, and it may (most likely) turn into financial debt as well.

Memories of too much heat, cold, or hunger as a child, causes unhappiness as an adult. Adverse comfort conditions cause us to respond, and in our responses, we put our mind on doing that which will appease or satisfy the *flesh*. We take our minds off godliness and put them on the things that pertain to *life*. Who is thinking about God when something is really hurting or aching? We all should be. I am talking about the very slightest discomfort where we make haste to give our flesh what it wants. Real or perceived discomfort is the impulse to **flesh works** that create debt, either spiritual, physical and/or financial.

Generational curses are the explanation as to why little Jimmy turned out the way he did even though you did **<u>EVERYTHING</u>** to help him be successful in life. You did everything in the **<u>natural</u>**, but what did you do about Jimmy's *spiritual inheritance*? Little Jimmy inherited DEBT, not the national deficit kind, but spiritual debt. He's as surprised as you–, or more.

How Can We Know?

Many have not received sound doctrine about debt, *the money kind* and the *spiritual kind*. Most are limited by the knowledge, agenda, or timidity of the preachers/teachers in the church. Folks can limit themselves by a lack of discipline to attend church on a regular basis to receive and apply even the limited teachings. We must seek Godly teaching on this subject and ask for Wisdom to correctly use what we learn.

Preacher Talk

Possibly you don't want to do it God's way. You hear the preacher, but you think that's just *preacher talk*. Don't miss God for looking at the preacher, thinking it's only a man's words. If you don't believe your pastor hears from God, you may need to find a new pastor. I didn't say your pastor doesn't hear from God, I said, *If **you** don't believe he or she hears from God.*

You may be right, or you may need God to renew a right spirit in you.

If you *know* that your pastor doesn't hear from God; then you need a new pastor. You can't say anything is wrong with the preacher--, necessarily, because *you* don't believe. The preacher could be right on target. It could just be that you don't *want* to hear what **God** is saying to you through that man or woman of God. The problem could be you. It could be that your pastor is on point and you're in the wrong church.

Don't refuse me, Lord--, and help my debt--. If you refuse the legitimate pastor or any person in spiritual authority over you, even a Godly request maybe denied if you are in rebellion. God has called you to submit to the pastor's leadership and you should submit to the anointing.

You never, ever have to submit to the pastor's **flesh**. The pastor should not ever bring that to church, but we are all human.

Because of spiritual rebellion God told Samuel that the people hadn't rejected Samuel by asking for a king instead of being satisfied with the judge, but that the people had rejected ***God***.

A Deacon of a certain church said that no man can tell him anything. That means he has no teachers, no preacher, no pastor; he hears no prophets. He will not be edified, exhorted, or comforted by Rhema, Words of Wisdom or Knowledge. He says only **God** can tell him anything. Scary. He's a long time Deacon in that church, a role model, a teacher and a counselor. Yet, this man isn't hearing the audible voice of God, either.

He is in full, covert rebellion. Few know his attitude about being pastored, corrected, or exhorted. The rest know nothing of it or his ongoing iniquity-- his *David sins* that he brags about when off church property.

On his ***assigned*** Sunday, he unashamedly reads and stumbles through a seven- or eight-line, 18th century prayer, from an index card while heads are bowed, and eyes are closed.

*Y*ou're still sitting under *that*? As long as you've decided to sit there and not grow spiritually, what do you think God is planning to do with you, or *for* you?

Because you're related to people in a church or by tradition doesn't mean you should stay there. That's the kind of church where you should put on the whole armor of God **just to**

go in there to protect yourself from spiritual regression.

God can place you in any situation for a season and for a reason. If you feel, or better -- *know* it is not God and the season is not God, then it's time to seek God and move on.

Poverty Is Not Holy

The Bible reads that in the last days, even the very elect would be deceived if it were possible. Thank God, that's not possible.

Who's doing the deceiving? Those who themselves are deceived, those who are in error, those who want to deceive others for personal gain, or those with an *I-got-mine-you-worry-about-yours* mentality.

There are those who are deceived into believing that poverty is holy. If poverty is so holy, **why do poor people commit so many crimes**? And why aren't all rich people just horrible?

Many saved and unsaved believers have been taught that money is dirty, so they go into underworlds and darkness to get this dirty money by gambling or drug-dealing for example. They want money; they *need* money, but they believe that is bad, so they go to bad places to get it so they can live comfortably in their lifestyles. If they have been taught properly that God wants us to prosper, and they should not be risking their life, health, peace and committing their own souls to hell—creating MORE DEBT (sin debt) to get *money*. The justification may be that they are not *stealing* money from the casino; that is being given to them (won), but because there is an idol *god* over gambling, they are in essence worshipping at that altar when they spend money there and creating *sin debt.*

God gives us power to get wealth; we don't have to sneak around for it. We do not have to do lowlife or underworld things to live or live abundantly. He does not lead us into temptation.

Let no man say when he is tempted, I
am tempted of God.

James 1:13a

The need for money will never justify sin or lifestyle choices because God has provided a way for us to be provided for, so we do not have to sin. Scriptures say, *choose life,* (Deuteronomy

30:19). There is **one life**. There are not *choices* of *life*. **If it's not of God, it's not a lifestyle, it's a death style**. If it's not of God, it will end in <u>death</u>. You may think you're living it up or living large, but while sinning either undercover or boldly in the open, you've actually chosen how you want to *die*. Don't be deceived.

When curses are running rampant, God has to refuse. Choosing God comes with promises. Sin life has fine print that we are counting on our 5-fold ministry gifts to teach us about. We can also read for ourselves in the Bible; **so why don't we know?**

Sometimes God is refusing you so you can see:

- That you're doing things wrong.
- **His Way**
- The poorness of your choice.
- You're out of order.
- He's not going to bless you until you are back in order.
- To save you trouble or your life.

Lord, Cancel My Debt

Turn to me and have mercy on me, as you
always do to those who love your name.
Psalm 119:132

    The debt-cancelling nature of God is
real. Sin is something that God can't look at,
but at Salvation and because of Mercy He can
cancel the debt of sin with your repentance,
confession of the sin and turning away from it.
How much more will He cancel the few dollars
you owe in the natural if you walk upright
before Him? It takes faith and resistance not to
renew old curses.

    **God doesn't look on sin, but He
looked on financial debt many times in the**

Bible. The widow woman whose two sons were about to be taken from her. The man who lost the axe head. **When God couldn't look on sin, He sent someone who could--, Jesus.** God's ultimate purpose in His love toward us is to keep us in a state where He **can** look on us. How can God minister to you, bless you, and keep you if He can't look at you?

When defiled, God cannot look on us. Defilement comes by blatant sin, and sneaky ways the devil defiles man or gets man to *defile himself* to keep him from the eyes and blessings of God. Works of the flesh *are* **sins** (Galatians). Food sacrificed to idols, which we may be blind to, too often is an abomination in God's eyes and defiles us. **This includes EATING in the DREAM.** Defilement includes sex in the dream among other things.

Fortunately, every morning *new mercies*, (Lam 3:22), so the defilement only lasts a day, with man's repentance and turning back to God. This explains why you will have another eating-in-the-dream dream; the devil is **renewing** the covenant, the curse, the defilement as soon as he can.

To not be refused by God, **choose God. Choose life. Work wisely and diligently to not be defiled.**

Lord, look upon us from heaven, where you live in your holiness and glory. Where is your great concern for us? Where is your power? Where are your love and compassion? Do not ignore us.
Isaiah 63:15 GNT

Getting Saved Is a Battle

Arise, and thresh .... And thou shalt beat in
pieces many people, and I will consecrate
their gain, and to the Lord and their
substance, and to the Lord of the whole
Earth. Micah 4:13

Getting saved is a battle. Being saved is a victory over evil; it's a victory over strongmen, spiritual wickedness, devils, and demons, generational curses and iniquity. It is a victory over debt, even if it's not realized fully at that exact moment.

Where there's a battle, there will be a victor. To the victor go the spoils. Spoils of battle can be substantial and when received, money or other value in the spoils can be used to retire debt in the natural.

Consecrate Your Gain

Bring the money into the storehouse so that
there may be meat in mine house.

Malachi 3:11

There's no shortage of money in the Earth, and especially not in God's hands. But God uses consecrated money that is brought in by obedient children of God. When there is powerful flow of consecrated money, it's easier for God to bless you.

Even if your money is a little bit of money, consecrate it to the Lord so He can use it to both bless the Kingdom and you. You get bread for your daily needs and seed will be multiplied back to you. How does God do this? I don't trouble myself with how, I just know THAT God does this. He can use any number of methods, paths, people and do it immediately and quickly or slowly and miraculously. He's God. I don't tell God what to do, instead, I do what God says. Amen.

I believe that by this time God is intended for us, as a whole, to have bought much more increase and gain into the House of God than we have, for consecration. He has told us, and expected us to arise, get up and thresh, go reap your harvest.

God intended for us to work in His garden, in His fields, sowing and reaping according to the Word. And God has intended for us to do much more in working the fields that are white to harvest. Because of sin we were dismissed or cast out of Eden where God intended for man to work in the Garden at Eden. And in return, that Garden would have provided. Instead, man is in the world, working the world's field. This is why so many people hate their jobs. They recognize they are out of the Garden, out of God's presence, or worse, out of God's will. Their joy in reaping is gone.

Not so for the son or daughter of God. We are in His realm, in His world. We are in this world but not *of* it. Because of sin, the punishment has been to work the world's system. That has netted man lot of labor with little to no reward, including the intangibles that go with satisfaction.

God still prospers His own and allows us to reap in joy as we also work His system. If it were not for sin and disobedience, we would be completely and entirely in God's system. Looking into the Scriptures, the 1000 years peace shows all men working at 100%, and in a Godly economy--, what God intended all along.

And they shall build houses and inhabit them, and they shall plant vineyards and eat the fruit of them. (Isaiah 65:21)

When you get past paying the 10%, then you can move into offerings. When God accepts an offering, He consecrates it. Ten percent, 100% and everything in between. So, wherever you get it, if you obeyed God and reaped it, harvested it, or got it from spoils, *without worshipping idols and false little g, gods,* God will sanctify and consecrate your gain.

Lottery Money

God doesn't want lottery money in the offering plate. *Or does He?* I've been preached to all my life that God condemns gambling and will not honor offerings gotten by illegal, immoral, or sinful means.

In the Book of Matthew, the priests are adamant about not putting *blood money* in the treasury. The money that Judas got for betraying Jesus that he threw on the temple floor was used to buy a potter's field, but not put in the offering. A potter's field is a place for the burial of strangers, then, and in our day, paupers. Blood money is cursed money.

Every dollar *ain't* a good dollar.

You haven't sold Jesus, thank God. But what can God do with money that you have not made a career or regular habit of getting in unbiblical ways but this time there may be *circumstances,* or some *creativity* involved in the getting of the money in your possession? What can we, what should we do with the kind of money that may not have been gotten in the godliest way? Do we throw it down in the temple like Judas and run out and get a rope? No.

You need a Word from God, either in Scripture or a Rhema, now-Word regarding the offering you desire to bring into the House of God for consecration. Ideally, ask God **first** if how you're planning to get it is okay, if you are not receiving increase by traditional channels, ask if increase from that particular method will be accepted.

Is sin involved in getting the money? *Thou shalt not steal.* Thou shalt not covet. *Sin money is ill-gotten gains.* If it's sin-money, blood money, don't accept it, give it back, repent. Talk to God about it. Dirty money is unconsecrated money**.**

Is there such as thing as money that <u>cannot</u> be consecrated? God rejects offerings that are blemished, imperfect, and/or involve sin. For example, there are some demonic items that have enchantments on them that cannot be "prayed away" or "prayed off"; they are unredeemable and must be destroyed and discarded.

Can we get money out of the kingdom of darkness at gunpoint, bring it to the feet of God and ask Him to bless it? No, we don't wrestle with human beings, but against spiritual wickedness. Offerings from spoils from *spiritual warfare* is acceptable to God. Unless God has **told** us to go to *war* against a people (a nation), that you hurt or robbed someone is the sin. If that sin is in you, it's working because of *iniquity*. Messing over anyone's money is another sin. Cheating people regarding money is a no-no; God hates a false balance. David said he could not bring an offering to God that cost him nothing. David is talking about gifted money, but I'm talking about stolen money, far worse. Stolen money is not earned money and does not make a proper offering.

And the king said unto Araunah, Nay; but I will surely buy it of thee at a price: neither will I offer burnt offerings unto the LORD my God of that which doth cost me nothing. (2 Samuel 24:24).

Is *all* money redeemable?

Everything an unrighteous life offers to God is a waste. Every work an unrighteous life does for God is an empty and unacceptable exercise.

Joseph Ola Okunola

God won't refuse an offering given with the right heart. God evaluates not only the offering, but also <u>*who*</u> is bringing the offering; the man with the right heart, the right spirit is *in, that man's offering is accepted*. The offering of a man with a corrupt heart won't be received. Cain v. Abel? Cain's heart was evil; he proved that when he **killed** his brother. A carnal man is at risk of being/becoming a devil agent. God said, *Esau have I hated* (Romans 9:13). Esau was a carnal man who also wanted to kill his brother, Jacob. God can read the intentions of our hearts, even when we haven't yet acted on evil impulses. The condition of our hearts, our character, our soul's prosperity affect whether or not offerings are accepted by the Father.

At odds with your brother? God doesn't accept that offering, either. Just as every dollar is not a good dollar to us, God operated that way, first. He does not accept every offering. If we follow God's lead it will keep us out of trouble.

This could be why there's **debt** in your life and why God doesn't seem to be answering your prayers, another reason for no return of 30, 60 or 100-fold that would greatly help you in life and also to pay off financial debt.

Let's say there wasn't *sin* involved, what you do with the money that's now in your hands? Consecrate it to the LORD. If the first fruit be holy, the lump is also holy, and if the root be holy, so are the branches, (Romans 11:16).

The term, *first fruit* is sometimes used interchangeably as the tithe, but they are not the same thing. The first fruit is the *first* of the harvest. It is considered the best of a crop. The first male child is also considered first fruit. We are to bring ten percent to God, first, not on the back end of our giving because of this people may think the first fruit in the tithe are the same thing. When the tithe is brought into the House of God first, it will not only be made holy, but it will also make the entire paycheck holy. Ideally it should be brought in first, but it is not necessarily first fruit.

A saint should have *holy* money. Everything about a saint should be holy. The tithe is 10% of the gross salary. When you get your tax refund money next year, you want it already consecrated, so tithe on your gross pay this year. Tithing on your net pay means you are giving unto Caesar *first* and apportioning out to God from the leftovers. If you just tithe on what you bring home, you might try to justify paying all your bills first and then tithe on the $20 you have left over after you meet all your obligations. That won't do. God gives you the power to get ***all*** the money you earn.

Just because taxes and expenses are taken out of your check before you see it doesn't mean you don't have to tithe on your gross. Let God bless **all** your money, especially your tax money. Didn't Jesus provide tax money out of the fish's mouth? Matthew 17:27. God wants to be in your tax money too, and in many cases, we need Him to be.

Why else are we bringing the money into the House except to sanctify it for both Kingdom use and so the money will be a blessing to us and not a curse? Your money must be sanctified. A real Giver wouldn't mind bringing all their money into the house for consecration, but you don't have to. Bringing 10% is the same as bringing **all** to God. That's very convenient because in Bible times bringing in one sheep could sanctify the whole flock. Bringing in one cow would sanctify the pasture and bless the entire ranch. That 10% principle really cuts down on the number of livestock in church.

However, bringing 10% of your family to church doesn't sanctify the whole house. A ratio of 10% saved, 90% unsaved will not get 100% of your household into Heaven.

Coin Fish

Then saith he unto them, Render therefore
unto Caesar the things which are Caesar's;
and unto God the things that are God's.
Matthew 22:20-21

Give unto Caesar that which is Caesar's.

The money in the fish's mouth came from the water kingdom (another whole book). This money was given to Caesar, whose image or inscription was on it. Was it consecrated first? Was it consecrated just by being in Jesus' presence? Was it consecrated by a Word from Jesus? Was it consecrated because Jesus was *aware* of it? Did it *need* to be consecrated since, according to Jesus it *belonged* to Caesar?

The money that Judas Iscariot threw on the Temple floor was NOT put in the offering, so it was NOT consecrated, but it was used by the priests. FOOD sacrificed to idols should never enter the temple of the Holy Spirit, which is your body. In the same way, **money** used in the sacrifice or worship of idols should never enter the church. The enchantment on somethings cannot be "prayed off." Blood money does not go in God's offering.

Satanic money does not belong in God's offering, so why would any human attempt to facilitate that? Elijah's altar **consumed** the evil altars of 450 prophets of Baal--, completely consumed them. Elijah didn't consecrate them or convert their use. Jesus can heal, renew, consecrate; God declares if a thing is redeemable or not. In giving, the person must come with a contrite heart and a broken, repentant spirit. Blood money is attached to pride, sin and other flesh works. Those offerings are not accepted.

When we do the work of an evangelist, we fish for men. Souls won to Salvation often give of their wealth. Yes, they do. When you minister spiritually to a lost soul, they will automatically offer you what they have. Even sinners see the great spiritual value of what they got versus the earthly things and stuff which have no eternal weight or value and they quickly donate, trade, or give. A cup of water, a Rolls Royce--, it's really a thing, so why it's not automatic for a Christian to give is a mystery to me.

Are Christians jaded? Greedy? Taking God for granted? The newly saved freely give. The first church at Antioch, for example, had *all things in common*. They stopped caring about STUFF.

In life, some things are not just handed over to you. Some things you have to *go get*. We have spiritual battles and take spoils from the nations, the *little k* kingdoms (spiritual nations) that have stolen from us.

Arise and thresh, O Daughter of Zion…thou shalt beat in pieces many people: and I will consecrate their gain unto the LORD, and their substance unto the Lord of the whole earth. Micah 4:13

The problem is not as much <u>WHERE</u> you get this money. The problem is <u>HOW</u> you get it.

Jesus didn't participate in raffles, sweepstakes, casino, lottery games or the drawing of straws because there is an evil entity ruling over all that, *Asmodeus* who is a prince of demons and hell.

Jesus *spoke* to the fish and the fish gave up its wealth. Two Disciples went and got the coin out of the fish's mouth. The fish obeyed; Jesus did not worship at any strange altar to get that coin, nor did He ever worship at any strange altar.

<u>HOW</u> you **get** the spoils is critical. Our example right now is gambling: **Do you *participate* in the games to win?** That's where the danger is because when you put money on the table, you are worshipping at the altar of that false *god*, that gambling *god*, Asmodeus. In so doing you are bowing to that idol *god*.

Where you put your money is where you <u>worship</u>. Where your treasure is, there will be your heart also, (Matthew 6:21). Money represents the fruit of your labor, it represents your life, your blood. Money is a serious sacrificial offering. Money is not to be worshipped, but it is used in worship.

Anything that **adds** to your spiritual debt cannot be an offering that would cancel, payoff, or retire natural debt. God will never compel you to rob a bank to get money for grandma's surgery, nor would He accept an offering from stolen money.

When worshipping an idol *god* you give your God-given grace to an evil entity and form an evil alliance. Demons like to cling onto a willing human; they need a human body to operate in the Earth, because they have no body. *Tag*! **Don't be it**. If you are willing to sin, they will hang on stubbornly. So when God wants to deal with that evil *idol*, or entity **even on your behalf**, He is hindered because **YOU** with your powerful self are in *alliance* with it.

You've got to stop. Repent. Break ties with and divorce all *idol gods--, sooner than later.* So, when they run you over **and they will if you don't get God in your life** God will be able to help you. Too many deceived people think they are as powerful or more powerful than the demon(s) that they let into their life. As long as you don't get into cahoots with a demon, you have authority over it. When you think you *partner* with it is when you lose what authority you have. At that point a man is subject to be run over by spiritual wickedness that he thought he could *train* like a genie in a bottle so he would have "powers" that others wouldn't have.

People, if devils were nice genies, why would they be locked away in hell needing to be summoned up by the evil, ignorant, and unsuspecting?

These demons keep you from God. Jesus could escort the robber on the cross beside Him into paradise because he accepted Jesus before he died; that repentant robber will be WITH Jesus. The other robber wanted to stay *with* whatever idol *god* he was serving, and so that other man would not/could not come into paradise. Evil idol devils, like barnacles or parasites attach to man, when that happens, that man will **NOT** *Enter **In*** to the presence of God, paradise, blessings, or Heaven.

We may get *in* after we get that evil off of us, not <u>*with*</u> it--, as long as we don't wait too long. Do it now while you have breath! After death when a person realizes they are being escorted to the torments of the darkest, hottest, burning hell with no way to return or repent; it's too late then. Can't change your mind then, the die is cast.

Do not form alliances with evil. If blinded by greed or lust you may think this "entity" will bring you power, luck, fame, fortune. Maybe so in the short-term, maybe not; they lie all the time. But you have to give up **everything**--*eventually*. That alliance will cost you **everything** in the long run, and for generations the debt of it will ruin your entire bloodline.

If you sin, repent quickly, do not let that sin and all the demons that come with it linger and become embedded in your life. This is what racks up debt, both spiritually and in the natural.

In gambling, for example, when you play their "shell game"—where you are given counterfeit promises of getting so much, and so much more for putting down so little, it's a game of *distraction*, something is being <u>stolen</u> from you—something more than the $1 or the $5. you put up to get in the game. While you are watching the cups, the ball, the wheel--, whatever you're gazing at that is hypnotizing you, while you lust for the win, a <u>spiritual transference</u> is happening. It may be imperceptible to you, possibly painless. This is true of all other sins of "pleasure" as well. You are being distracted in the natural while being ripped off in the spirit. Sooner or later you will realize it in the natural.

When the woman with the issue of blood touched the hem of Jesus' garment, He said that **virtue** had flowed from Him. **WHY DON'T WE HUMANS FEEL IT WHEN <u>VIRTUE</u> LEAVES US?**

Virtues are the gifts, skills, abilities or good qualities that God has given you. Any commendable quality, strength or courage that makes you who you are. Virtue also is needed in your purpose and to reach your destiny.

I had an unsaved, fake friend who had the oddest timing, she seemed to always call me as soon as I was through praying. Prayers of the righteous makes power available to us. She'd call, and suck the anointing, the virtue out of me. I didn't feel it as it was happening, but most often **after** her call I would feel flat spiritually, or drained. You know what I'm talking about, some people just *take it out of you.* That connection is OVER.

We may not notice that virtue is gone until we don't walk in divine favor anymore--, or, shunned where we used to be accepted. We are reproached where people used to celebrate us. Grades in school may go down, all the way to failing and you can't get into the college you want. Or, we may have no peace in our lives. It could be that a marriage breaks up, a family is lost. Worse, people could die.

Then we notice – you final notice that ever since _____ (fill in the blank), your life changed. Jesus, of course could recharge far better than we could, but we can get our virtues and anointing back. We can get into proper connection with God again and protect ourselves from spiritual vampires. You know, those who you hope want to be saved so you minister to them only to find out they are just using you to "feel better."

Prove Me

And when the Queen of Sheba heard the fame of Solomon concerning the name of the Lord, she came to prove him with hard questions. (1 Kings 10:1)

The first queen spoken of in the Bible was the Queen of Sheba, who came from Africa (or Asia) to see King Solomon. This Queen came to *prove* the king. As a queen, she had right position to have an audience with the king, and she came to ask him hard questions. If you are ignorant or insecure about who you are, you will not come into the presence of royalty. You must feel worthy.

When you worship God as king, you are promoted to royalty because you are His child.

When you know you are royalty, you are comfortable to be in His presence.

Even if you somehow manage an audience with the King, but don't realize who you are. You will not ask Him hard questions such as, *Father, will you heal me? Father, will you provide for me? Father, will you bless me, help my debt?* Of course, as royalty you should not be in debt, but we all know debt relief can be a process.

Sheba came bearing gifts. You don't come into the presence or attempt to come into the presence of a king without a gift. You don't go to church without an offering. You don't attempt to enter into or receive from the presence of God without a worthy, unblemished gift.

You expect to go to Heaven? What do you plan to bring to the very throne of God as a gift? Have you thought about it? Your works? Are they fireproof? Will you be able to *present* them to God?

Sheba became to prove Solomon with hard questions, for he was full of Wisdom. How much more is.

- Our God, full of Wisdom.
- Our God, full of healing.
- Our God, full of wealth.
- His name? A strong tower.
- He full of grace and mercy.
- He savior.
- Our God, full of blessings.

God says, ***"Prove Me."*** God is not planning to refuse you. He is inviting you, drawing you, and giving you permission to come to Him. Proving God will cause God to have to give out what you are asking and believing Him for. The Scriptures say, we can come boldly to the Throne of Grace, (Hebrews 4:16). *That* you don't know you can go to God says that you don't worship, and you are not accustomed to being in His presence. But you can change all that; become a worshipper. Become a prayer warrior, boldly at the Throne of Grace and in His presence, knowing who you are, worshipping and having brought an acceptable gift, you can ask God, *"Lord, help my debt."* No matter what kind of debt, God is able.

Can you imagine how God must feel? What He must be thinking sometimes? There He is, Wonderful, Awesome, Mighty and Blessed, but people still don't believe in Him. So, He says, **PROVE ME. I WANT TO SHOW YOU THAT I AM REAL. I WANT TO SHOW YOU THAT I AM GOD. I WANT TO SHOW YOU THAT *I AM*.**

God doesn't want to be invisible any more than you'd want to be invisible to your children or loved ones. He wants to be real to you and to me. God is real, and He invites us to ***prove*** Him.

Bring ye all the tithes into the storehouse …prove me now here with saith the Lord of host, if I will not open you the windows of heaven and pour you out of blessing. There shall not be room enough to receive it.
Malachi 3:10

This *proving* requires some steps on your part. God will not reveal Himself to someone who doesn't want to see Him. When you bring your tithes and offerings into the House of God, it is an act of worship. You are saying, *"God, reveal Yourself to me. I want to see You."*

When you come boldly to the throne of petition or worship, you're asking God the same thing and He will open up Heaven and pour you out blessings. What are those blessings? They are whatever you need. If you need healing, God won't send you a new house unless you're sick of the old one. Debt cancellation? Yes, God can do that too. God sends you what you need and what you ask for. He *reveals* Himself in the attribute that you have faith for and need.

> He that hath my commandments, and keepeth them, he it is that loveth me, and he that loveth me shall be loved of my father, and I will love him and will manifest myself to him. (John 14:21)

No one brings gifts to God unless they believe that He really exists. And folk don't part easily with something they want for themselves if they don't believe, if they don't have faith. Whether or not you have faith is revealed in your actions toward God.

In the *proving*, a sinner will ask for a sign. No wonder, huh?

In the *proving* a stranger will ask for ID. *God, is that You?* If you don't know His ways, His voice and His touch then you don't yet know Him. Do you know the sound of your natural father's voice and other characteristics about him? That's how it should be with God; He should be that real to you.

In the *proving* a believer will ask for a Word. He sent His Word and healed them, (Psalms 107:20).

In the *proving* a son or daughter will simply make room for the blessing.

Literally, the Shunammite woman built a *room* for the prophet. In so doing, she made room for her own blessing--, her son, (2 Kings 4:8-37).

I don't have to tell you which one you are, just read the above 4 descriptions again and find yourself. If you're not yet a son or a daughter, that is your goal. *Don't refuse me, Lord. Lord, help my debt.* God does not refuse the abiding requests of His sons and daughters.

For if you abide in me, and my words are biting you. We shall ask what you will, and it shall be done unto you, (John 15:7).

A Gourd or a Tree

The sun shall not smite me by day, nor the moon by night. The Lord shall preserve thee from all evil. He shall preserve thy soul. The Lord shall preserve thy going out and thy coming in from this time forth, and even forevermore. Psalms 121:6-8

God grew Jonah an overnight gourd to shelter him from the blazing sun after Jonah had prophesied to Nineveh, (Jonah 4). We will not discuss why the gourd was struck down almost as quickly as it grew up. But the purpose of this conversation is to ask you one question: A gourd or a tree? What do you need?

Either a gourd or a tree can be used for protection or shade. Which one depends on what you need it for, when you will need it and for how long. You may not know, but God knows what you need, when you need it, for how long, and for what reasons. He will provide if you let Him. He knows all of your life and He can plan for you better than you can for yourself.

Are you asking God for something, such as more money, or debt cancellation? You may have asked Him times before for this same thing. It's been years. You sowed the seed. It may have been a sizable offering that really stretched your faith and shrunk your wallet. But you knew it was God, so you obeyed cheerfully. You trust God, yet you're still waiting. What's taking so long?

God's Growing a Tree

Jonah's gourd grew overnight, but trees don't.

It's been so long. Many Christians do not wait for their seeds to develop and grow. They do not wait for their blessings to reach maturity before snatching the seeds out of the ground, ripping fragile seedlings from nurturing soil, or renouncing the offering sown and killing it. God is taking too long? When you go into your flesh, those flesh works kill spiritual seeds.

In the world, many pay penalties for early withdrawal of investments. They want their savings account money *now*. Or to use retirement money for now-purchases. I've seen people who can't get their pension money any other way than to quit their jobs prematurely. So, they do.

In God, we shouldn't be this way. We should not be anxious for anything. We have to learn to trust God when it comes to the trees and the gourds He's growing for our protection, shade, or provision. If we are developing the Fruit of the Spirit called long-suffering, patience should be a piece of cake.

Different Seeds

Although they may look the same to you, gourd and tree seeds are different. How deep you plant a seed depends on how long it takes for that particular seed to germinate. God may have a gourd grow for you if you need shade for a day or two at some time in your near future. But if you need a full tree to sustain you in the distant future for an extended time, leaves for healing, fruit for nourishment, wood for warmth or housing, and more seeds for sowing, God provides just that.

Allen was in legal straits concerning a matter that had lingered in the court system for over a year. He had exhausted the expertise of his current attorney, who, even with prayer and intercession, did not represent him well. By coincidence, Alan met an old friend in the mall whom he had not seen in 20 years. As they reminisced about their past the attorney remembered the kindness that Alan had shown him before he had moved away to college. Allen had no idea his former schoolmate was planning to be a lawyer, had been to law school, or had come back home to practice law. Allen only remembered that his friend had moved several states away a score of years ago. This friend was now an attorney who specialized in just the problem with which Allen needed expertise.

Allen's, acts of friendship to the then-student, now-lawyer, and spiritual and financial faithfulness to God had planted seeds that allowed God to grow Allen a tree. If Alan had been anxious, greedy or doubtful, he could have panicked, gone into the flesh, and stopped being faithful in tithing and offerings, but he didn't. Alan kept the faith by saying, *God, I know you can help me. I know you're going to bless me. I may not know how you're going to do it, but I know you're going to do it.* That's how you keep the faith.

Alan had sowed seeds, counting them as dead. He had also forgotten about the seeds of kindness and friendship sown so long ago. That seed had been growing for 20 years. Just when Alan really had a need, God sent a mighty tree to sustain him and give him a legal victory.

If you are an obedient Sower and a faithful and cheerful giver, then you have a serious crop in the ground. God can give you an extension to pay your debt by providing a gourd tomorrow, or a tree that you may not know about has grown, is filled with fruit and there is a harvest waiting for you, correlating to your relationship with God, your spiritual walk and worship of the LORD of the Harvest.

God has grown trees and gourds for you all your life. Would you rather that God bless you with $1000. tomorrow or $1,000,000. in a few years? Depends, doesn't it? You might really need that $1000. more today than $1,000,000 later. Sometimes it matters more *when* you get money than how much it is. What and where you receive depends on where, what and how much you've sown.

Your Crop

The flax and barley were destroyed, since the barley had headed and the flax was in bloom. The wheat and spelt, however, were not destroyed, because they ripen later.

Exodus 9:31-32 NIV

Your spiritual financial portfolio should be diverse, similar to what your investment banker or financial planner might have helped you establish. Some of your seed is still in the ground, while other seed is growing, maturing, and other is being harvested. The hailstorm referenced in the above passage from Exodus destroyed the barley and the flax, but the wheat and the rye were not yet grown up, so they were not hurt.

All plants have different growing seasons and different hardiness. Some seeds grow slower than others. Some fruit can mature and keep on the vine, (*hold*) until needed and stay preserved. God knows; He is the Master Gardener who can establish your spiritual and financial portfolio better than any stockbroker or investment planner can establish your financial portfolio. That doesn't mean don't use the services of financial planners but put your ultimate faith in God. Pray about anyone who manages, invests or even touches your money.

The Lord is thy keeper, the Lord is thy shade upon thy right hand. Psalms 121:5

For as the rain cometh down in the snow from heaven, and returneth not thither but watereth the earth, and make it to bring forth and bud, that it may give seed to the sower, and bread to the eater. Isaiah 55:10

Seeds are very handy. They can be carried around in your pocket. You can carry an entire orchard in a packet, in your pocket. With seeds, like Abraham, you can carry a nation inside of you. God put seeds in a cool dark place--, *in you*. Those seeds await the water of the Word, the Light of Jesus Christ, and the heat of the Holy Spirit. When we don't become the thing that God intends us to be, the seeds don't germinate because becoming what we should *become*, brings life to the seed. No seed will grow without water, warmth, and a light to reach toward. When the water of the Word, the warmth of one another, the Love and the Light of Jesus is in you, your seeds germinate and grow.

Sometimes it seems God is taking a long time to bless you. **It may be so you won't worship the gift you receive instead of God who gave the gift**.

God wants to prosper us. The NT tells us that He is Lord of the Harvest.

Pray ye therefore the Lord of the Harvest. He will send forth laborers into his harvest,

(Matthew 9:38, Luke 10:2)

Harvest is the time when you reap the benefits of your work, the benefits of having planted, cultivated; watered and *not fainting,* (Galatians 6:9.)

God says that He reaps at His coming.

Are you looking to reap? Are you looking for God? You should be. Are you accusing God of not being in your situation? Then accuse Him no more, if you are reaping, God is there--, whatever you're reaping. Fish? Produce? Prosperity in your business? God is there.

Nevertheless, at thy word I will let down the net. And when they had done this. They enclosed a great multitude of fishes and their net broke, (Luke 5:16)

Before they had the Word of God, they had all the seeds: the boat, the water, the nets and the manpower. But there was no great harvest because Jesus was not yet there. When Jesus arrived and at His Word, prosperity was realized.

Or are you harvesting fishes and loaves? Are you harvesting natural and *spiritual* food?

And when he had taken the five loaves and the two fishes, he looked up to heaven, and blessed, and break the loaves, …the two fishes divided he among them all. They did all eat and were filled and they took up 12 baskets full of fragments. And of the fishes, about five thousand

(Mark 6:41-44).

Two fish and five loaves became *seed* even on dry land. God was there, so there was much harvest.

Or is the evangelist in you seeking to reap or harvest men? God is there.

And so was also James and John, the sons of Zebedee. Which were partners with Simon and Jesus, said unto Simon, fear not, from henceforth thou shalt catch men. Luke 5:10

And if I be lifted? Up I will draw all men
unto me. *John 12:32*

When Jesus is lifted up in the Word
preached, when the Gospel is carried, then
reaping of men occurs. God arrives again as
the Word. You cannot win any man to Christ
without the Word of God. You cannot win
anyone to Christ with *your* words, only. With
your words you can win them to be *your*
followers or in your cult, but not to
Christianity.

And you know the purpose of reaping
men is winning souls, for the Kingdom, all to
the glory of God. You personally cannot admit
anyone to Heaven, so, they must be won to
Christ Jesus.

The devil, that Counterfeit is also trying
to reap souls for hell. Careful, people of the
Earth!

Growing Seasons

God doesn't need to watch the flowers
grow. That's your job, that's my job, and with

the beauty He's put in them, it's a blessing to watch them. Flowers and trees are quite obedient. You are chosen as the husbandmen over the vineyard He has planted. That's why you are here. Then God shows up for the glory. Adam and Eve were put here to dress the Garden at Eden. *Dressing* the Garden, doing what God put you here to do is **worship.**

At work, your boss gives an assignment, then the boss gets the glory as you show what your creativity and efforts have wrought. The boss provided the place, the materials, and sustained you to give him glory in front of the client. Your boss provided everything you needed to be successful: an office, phone, pens, paper, computer. Then you got paid when the work was done. That's what you're here for, to do the work. God **sustains** you as you work and give Him glory.

God expects to receive glory from the seeds you plant, cultivate, and prosper. That's one way you'll know it's of God by the glory *He* receives.

Glory of the Harvest

God shows up in the fullness of time, at maturity, perfection, and at completion. Jesus showed up in the fullness of time right when we needed Him. He showed up when you reaped Salvation for yourself. If you're reaping, God is there.

We have established that God gives seed and that you are to plant, water, and cultivate for your own blessings, all to the glory of God. What will you have to give based on the seed He has given you?

Prayer

I bless You, Lord. I bless Your holy Name. There's none like You. I love You, Lord. I trust Your system of planting, sowing, growing and reaping in Jesus' Name. Amen.

Exercise

Gourds God has provided.

Trees God grew for me.

How have I honored God for those gourds?

How have I honored God for those trees listed above?

Meditate on the fact that God is the shade on your right hand. You may have been, or maybe walking in shade that God has provided for you that you may not have been previously aware of.

Praise the Lord for all He has done for you.

Worship Him for who He is.

Forgive Us Our Debts

Take you the spoil of silver. Take the
spoil of gold, for there is none end of the
store and glory out of all the pleasant
furniture, (Nahum 2:9).

But what about the things that God has
blessed you with, that you *haven't yet
received*? If you have not met all the
conditions for having them, such as faith,
salvation, giving, et cetera, this could be why
you don't have them. Shouldn't you be
redeemed from debt by now?

Have those promised things been in
your hands, but they've been taken from you?
How were they taken? If so, what now?

What if God finally came through with
that promise He made to you, but you've been
ripped off by the devil or his agents in the

Earth? The good news is the stuff that's been stolen from you as you walked *among some thieves* can be returned.

The devil hates you. The devil steals, kills, and destroys. The devil wants to lead you into sin, to defile you. Once defiled you can be *accused* to God and the devil hopes to destroy you because God cannot look on sin. That is, God cannot look on the defiled. The surest way to have God look *away* from you is to sin, willfully and repeatedly. The devil loves it when a man is neck-deep or worse, in sin, transgressions, and *iniquity*.

While in sin you are still you. You are still gifted of God and still have value in the Earth. The act of sinning, which is usually considered something pleasurable by the sinner (else, he wouldn't do it), is the distraction the devil uses to steal from you. What does he steal? Any and everything he can. But he starts with gifts, skills, ability, favor--, God-given virtues. He starts out subtle and you may not notice these things.

Have you ever heard that sin makes you dumb? It does. It makes people dull, mentally and in other ways as well, (Ephesians 4:18). Sin darkens their understanding. It would be a shame to get all of that understanding from the Proverbs then turn around and lose it to sin. While sinning, a man's senses are dulled, spiritually, making it easier for the devil to rip him off.

The flesh is heightened during sin; sin is sensual. In the course of sinning, the focus is on the flesh instead of the spirit. Sin is exciting when you're thinking about it, planning it and doing it--, most of the time. That excited flesh is to distract you. Distraction: a common devil trick. Of course, the devil's promise to that sinner is that he'll get away with that sin. He won't, but he may be so excited to both do the sin and think he'll not be caught. A perfect devil storm.

In the natural and in the spirit, there are immediate and long-term results of sin. The immediate losses were mentioned above. The long-term loses are *death*. Death of something.

Death of some things. Death. Death of relationships, maybe even people. Whatever sin or devil deal a person thinks they are making that only involves them is never the case; it involves their bloodline. The debt and cost will involve their loved ones. A quick example: How many famous celebrities have tremendous losses in their lives and families? It's not so they will have a great story for the tabloids. **It is debt**. They may be rich in the natural, but spiritually, they owe. *Why are there so many troubled celebrities?*

Sin costs entirely too much! Longer-term consequences of sin are *long term* because it gets in a family, in a bloodline and keeps repeating and repeating like a broken record.

Before and after death, there is debt. Lord, help our debts. **Forgive us our debts as we forgive our debtors. Debts that remain after death are passed to your kids and grandkids.**

When you, or someone in your bloodline wakes up and becomes spiritual enough to receive the FULL redemption that Christ died for us to have, **stop sinning,** repent, and go back to purge your bloodline of the sin, evil covenants, curses and take back all the devil stole from you (bloodline), the *spoils* that you and your family will realize can be reaped.

The spoils are the goods and the stuff, anything of value taken in battle.

Sometimes the gifts, favor, et cetera that *was* to come to you never got to you because the devil interfered and STOLE them from you by getting you to sin before (sometimes right before) you were about to receive them.

We need the LORD of the Harvest so we can harvest, reap blessings because there are powers that do not want you to reap; they want to steal your blessings. We need the **power** to get wealth, power to *keep* wealth. We need God if we are reaping. Stupidly, when about to get paid, if we fall into pride and sin, that is as good as the devil wants it. Anger is a huge repellant of blessings. If you're an angry sort, or easily angered, take note if someone triggers you right before you are going to get a blessing or breakthrough.

Stop falling for it!

If you do not remain upright before the Lord, but instead fall down before the devil the devil may take what was to be yours right before you even get it. Right before you ever get it. If you do not acknowledge that there is a problem, that you sinned, and are therefore part of the problem, you will blame God and mess up your Christian walk. And that's what the devil wants.

If you don't know you've been ripped off by the devil, you won't do warfare. If you won't go into battle, or do spiritual warfare, then you won't recover spoils.

It's complicated. But it's doable.

The spoils are everything that you have been promised but have not yet received, such as health, family, spouse and children. The spoils are everything that has been withheld from you. Some of your blessings will come as spoils. Spoils will be things you had in the past that were taken from you by the devil.

Don't look down on hand me downs. Abraham's vast wealth was from spoils. David became a wealthy man because of spoils. With spoils, sometimes all you have to do is pick them up, but that's not the same as gleaning. What is to be gleaned is left in the fields, willingly by the person who grew the crops, corn, et cetera. Spoils are after a battle or a war. Spoils are sometimes left as the enemy is beaten or flees, but at other times the spoils must be taken right out of the enemy's hand, such as in the case of sickness and near-death infirmities.

Are you willing to do that? Are you willing to confront or engage the enemy to get your promises and blessings? That could be why you don't have them. Are you willing to take the spoils out of the devil's grip?

In your warfare **<u>REQUIRE</u>** the devil to return back to you all that he has stolen, 7-fold (or more) in the Name of Jesus. That is Scriptural.

This chapter is about the spoils, not the spoiled. It is not about those too lazy to advance the Kingdom or pursue and ignite the enemy. It is not about the spoiled, those who are used to someone doing everything for them.

As a saint of GOD, you should not be sinning, so you should not be racking up debt. I say – if you have lasting DEBT, it is because there is something else going on. Being a Christian does not make you broke, it should make you successful, wealthy. God gives wealth and establishes covenants with His people. How's your wealth? Your joy, your peace? Things such as these that have been stolen from you by the devil are spoils that need to be recovered by you. God has a way to get things back to us. God is trying to give you inheritance promises, things stolen, and even weapons previously used against you.

Take the enemy's weapons.

If you don't want a child to keep bombarding you with a water gun, take the toy pistol from him. Tired of the devil attacking you? God has a way to take the weapons that the devil's using out of his hand. Align yourself with God. Aren't you tired of it, had enough? If you're tired of devil beatings, align with God to take the weapons from the devil. Is your money funny? Where's the tithe? Where are your offerings? Is your money being used cleanly?

Is your health under attack? Are you eating well, drinking water and exercising? Are you staying up all night like the grown-ups and then getting up at the crack of dawn? No wonder you're tired. I am in no way suggesting that you go to sleep without praying. If you're up, by all means PRAY. A lot of weight is put on **midnight prayers**. Pray if you're up, or as soon as you get up. Interrupted sleep is not naturally beneficial, but man must always pray.

Resistance: Resist the Devil

Whatever you do, **don't help the devil.** You must resist the devil. When the devil uses a person to hurt you, if you do something back to that person, you also hurt *them*, not the devil. In so doing, you hurt God because that blatant sin *defiles* you and God can't look on you for that day. So, you hurt yourself **<u>TWICE</u>**. The original hurt (sin) and the debt for having sinned.

Next, that person may put your picture on the face of their known or unknown enemy. Then tag, you're it. It's 100% flesh. However, if you do nothing to them but get into spiritual warfare, God can get the devil off you and help the other person as well. I just thought I'd mention that.

Let's consider sickness and immunity to certain diseases. When a disease such as chickenpox presents itself to you, your body creates antibodies against the virus that causes the disease. If you have enough antibodies, you don't get the disease. If you don't have enough antibodies, you may get the disease, but while you're sick, you build up immunity to that disease. After you get over the disease, you now have *resistance* to it, which means you have antibodies to it now. Too late? No. Even if you get under attack by the virus that causes chickenpox again, it can't hurt you.

Spiritually, while going *through*, you build up knowledge, Wisdom, and faith. When/if that situation presents, again, you also have **spiritual immunity**, you know how to, and can resist it.

Chicken pox is a weapon previously used against you that you now have authority over. You may not use chicken pox as a weapon against the enemy. You can't give him the disease because he doesn't have a flesh body, but because of antibodies he can't use it against you again. Similarly, God has given us vaccines for chickenpox, shingles, mumps, measles, polio and covid, for example. We vaccinate ourselves and children so their bodies will make antibodies *in advance*. Then when/if the agent that causes anything that our children are vaccinated against comes up to try to make them sick, they already have resistance to the disease, and they don't get sick. The devil can't use those diseases against us anymore. Hallelujah.

The Bible says we are to submit to God, resist the devil, and the devil will flee, just as we physically resist disease by having something in us: antibodies before the assault even comes along. We can spiritually resist the devil by having something in us before temptations come, the Word and the Holy Spirit.

That's what worship and offerings are about. It is our way of reserving the things that God is going to give us. Worship and offerings pave the way in advance for the blessings. Are you tired of the devil attacking your body? Get mad, then get well. Make yourself some antibodies; he can't touch you then. God has put the capability in you already. It's called an immune system. We all have one. Further, we have dominion over our bodies, and we can tell our bodies and immune system *how* to serve us. Reject sickness, cast it out of your body in the Name of Jesus.

This is how to take the weapons

out of the devil's hands.

Are you tired of the accuser whispering in your ear that you're not good enough or they know what you did? *Then confess your sins.* Else the devil will blackmail and emotionally torment you forever. Confess. You don't have to tell anyone but God.

Take the weapon out of the devil's hand. Every time you sin and have sin and have not repented, you have given the devil an opportunity to choose a weapon against you. Every weapon he is using, you have given him permission, in a sense to pick up. Additionally, there may be some *generational* weapons that you need to take out of his hands as well (iniquity). And you do that by spiritual warfare.

You want Peace of Mind? Are you tired of the devil messing with you and your peace? Then get tough! Sister Rude, an undercover devil agent is on Pew two, there to offend you. She keeps staring at you and then when you look at her, she looks away, rolling her eyes. Get tough. Don't let her offend you; don't you dare come out of praise and worship. She obviously wasn't into any real worship, because in the presence of God is fullness of joy, not fullness of rudeness, not fullness of flesh, or fullness of rolling your eyes.

Witness Protection plan: Witness to the unsaved,

so the Blood of Jesus will protect them.

Whatever God has planned for you that you didn't get or whatever He gave you that was stolen, these are spoils. You can take spoils and use it against the despoiled. Your restored family is a spoil. Yes, people are spoils. How can you use your restored family against the devil? Get them in church and worship the Lord. Get them involved in ministry, get them in the Witness protection plan. **Teach them how to witness to the unsaved so they can become saved, and the Blood of Jesus will protect them**. People are spoils, folks once on the downside of life who have been snatched out of the grips of sin and death are spoils and their testimony will set others free, or at least give them hope.

God is mighty in battle, (Psalm 24). He graciously gives us spoils, everything of value taken in battle. You can retire a lot of debt with spoils of war.

Let me tell you about a battle. Jesus went to hell for us. He went down in hell to get some keys. While walking around He looked over and saw health, the devil had taken it. Jesus said, *"Give Me that; that's a spoil. I know some folks who can use that.* Then He saw wealth and He said, *"Give me that; that's a spoil. I'm going to give that to My people."* Then He saw peace, joy and happiness, all with your name on it. And He said, *"Give me that; that's a spoil. I know who that belongs to."*

"Then He saw Wisdom. *Devil, what are you doing with that down here? You don't even know how to work it. Give me that. If you knew how to work it, you'd read the book and find out that you're a defeated foe. Devil, you don't have a chance-- in hell."*

Jesus went to hell for some keys. He got them too, but He also got spoils. He saw Captivity and He said, *"I'll take that too."* Jesus came out of hell, having defeated Death. He came out of hell, victorious, and with spoils. **"See you, devil. Wouldn't want to be you."**

When He ascended up on high, He led captivity captive and gave gifts unto men. (Ephesians 4:8)

The Spoils

The battle is the Lord's, but He gives us the victory and the spoils. He won all power and authority, then gave it to us, (Luke 11:22). The Greater One is doing all this spoiling and shall ultimately spoil the devil. The Greater One is in me, the Greater One is in you. But you can only do what God tells you to do with the spoils, **You** can't decide because they are God's spoils. It all belongs to Him, ultimately.

What does God tell us or expect us to do with the spoils? The following:

- **Destroy all**. In the case of things accursed. If we spoil the drug dealer down the block, we don't keep the crack or sell it to users or addicts for profit. Destroy all, (Joshua 8) at Ai? There were plenty good spoils, *but God was not going to consecrate any of it.*

- **Destroy part** and keep part according to the Word of God. Some part of the spoil may be accursed, some may be consecrated to the Lord for the building of His Kingdom. It depends on what it is and what God says in that particular situation. God can use ill-gotten cash and consecrate for His use, but He doesn't consecrate that crack, LSD, marijuana and other harmful drugs, for example.
- **Keep all.** The wise stewards consecrated all to God to His glory.
- **Dedicate part of it to God**, for the victory Abraham gave the 10th part.

God gives us enough for the tithe, bread to the eater, seed to the sower, and multiplies seed sown, (Isaiah 55:10b). After we receive all that bread and seed, God wants and deserves our dedication.

There's glory in the spoils. If we give God His glory, He will give us our glory in the natural. We must admit that there's glory in spoils. The one with the most **stuff** *appears* to win. A divorce or war--, same thing. The one who comes out with the most tangible stuff *appears* to win. Divorce spoils are traditionally creature comforts such as houses, cars, jewelry, clothes, small children, and especially money. In reality, the one who comes out most balanced with the most peace actually wins. The real winner grows in the things of God and prospers over and above owning the dining set that the couple brought together in 1985.

There is rest in the spoils. If you know the enemy has no weapons to use against you, won't you sleep peacefully at night? Yes.

God wants our dedication. Great success calls for proportionate returns. Men of both natural and spiritual wars must honor God with the spoils. Where are the dedicated things to dedicate to Him? What is due Him in silver, gold, testimony, praise, worship, and time?

The Treasure House

The Treasure House, (Daniel 1:2) is where everything is laid up that we are *planning* to give **God**. The Treasurer took care of the stuff in the treasure house. Ideally, you should be so in love with God, so excited about what He has done for you, so honored to be able to praise, worship, adore, and bless Him that you have a storehouse, a treasure house of things from which to bless the Lord. It's Biblical. You're just waiting to bless Him. You don't have to borrow anything. You're not taken by surprise *that* you will worship God in your giving, since that is the purpose for living.

Yes, there is sacrificial giving, but worshipping God regularly should be in your plans.

How many of you have a special ring, necklace, or trinket that you're saving for your daughter when she becomes a teenager? Your family heirlooms are part of your treasure house. How many men are waiting to give your son great-grandfather's watch, or something of great spiritual, material or sentimental value? How about your family Bible? That's a treasure. That retirement account that you're planning to give *yourself* when you turn 65 is in your treasure house because you love yourself.

What's in your treasure house to God? Surely you love no man more than you love God. Where are the dedicated things?

I'm not saying to take your family heirlooms or retirement accounts to the church, except that God tells you. You love people dearly in your life, and you plan in advance to give them *things*, just as God has given us so much in advance. He's given us resistance to diseases, as discussed earlier. Mainly He gave us Jesus Christ before the foundation of the world. The more you love, the more you plan to give. **God put Jesus in a treasure house for you before the foundation of the world**. Don't you love God as much? Hopefully more.

Aren't you already planning what you will give your friend for her birthday, or your husband for Christmas? You may not have already gotten those gifts, but they are in your treasure house. Is it in your attic, or maybe your guest closet? The more you love a person, the more thoughtful you are toward them.

What has the Lord brought you through? What has He delivered you from? What has He set in your hand or restored to your possession? What victories has He given you? These are spoils. Remember the Lord your God, He is mighty in battle, and He gives us victory and spoils.

But it is written, eye has not seen, nor ear heard, neither have entered into the heart of man, the things which God hath prepared for them that love him. (1 Corinthians 2:9)

God has every Godly thing you've been wishing for, and more. All the spoils are His, and they are already in His treasure house for you because He loves you.

Prayer for the Spoils

Father, you've promised us so much in Your Word. We bless You, Lord; You are worthy of all praise, all honor, all the glory. You are so faithful to us, daily loading us with benefits. We are rich beyond measure in Christ. Thank You, Lord, for inheritance. Thank You for the blessings of provision and peace and joy. Thank you for divine help. Thank You, Lord, for giving us so much more than we deserve, by Grace.

We come against the enemy in the Name of Jesus. Empower us by Your Spirit to be victorious in spiritual warfare. Empower us to pursue and recover all, in the Name of Jesus. Everything that our Father has promised us, we receive it right now. We declare that those things that the Lord God has promised us are ours. Now we take back all that has been stolen from us. We reach out our hands and in faith we receive all the spoils of war that our Father has won for us and graciously given to us.

Thank You Lord, for restoration, peace, hope, Joy, health and wealth. Thank You for restoring our homes, families, jobs, and careers. We love You, Lord, and receive all the spoils of warfare to Your glory. So, when people in the world see us, they will know that we are children of the Most High God. And they will be drawn to You because they will see how You have not refused us, Amen.

Spiritual warfare takes more than just praying, but it does take praying. Now take action.

Exercise:

Begin to do what God instructs you. Or what He has instructed you to do in the past in order to receive the spoils. **Take action!**

Yield to God

What you yield to God, he can use, (2 Timothy 2:22). If God is using it, He's making something awesome of it. Ten percent is about what God calls a *remnant*; it is the leftovers to us. It's the little bit of stuffing remaining from the turkey dinner. It's the corner in the milk jug. It's the crumbs from the cake, and usually nobody wants it. Ten percent is the cream that rises to the top of whole milk, and it can be the cream of a crop. God loves the 10%; He can use it with the tithe, or even when it's a remnant. God's way is not to make patchwork quilts out of remnants like we do, but somehow, miraculously and divinely, He stretches it to wholeness again. In the Garden at Eden, He took a little rib and made a whole woman. The remnant of Israel was restored to a nation in the Book of Isaiah.

God took the remnant you had left of yourself when you got through with the world, or the world got through with you, and you finally accepted Salvation, and has restored you to wholeness as much as you have allowed Him.

Our 10% tithe is made whole again by the divine touch of God. God says He is Alpha and Omega, the Beginning and the End. He can bless us coming in and going out (Deuteronomy 28). It's amazing what He can do with only 10%.

Scientists say that man uses only 10% of his brain.

God First, Always

There's a pattern of brain waves called alpha waves. It is the predominant brain pattern when we are awake and relaxed. I call these alpha waves God waves because He is the Alpha and Omega. We should always be thinking of God *first*. He is the Alpha. When we are relaxed, we are resting in Him and allowing Him to work in and through us. Keeping our minds stayed on God is the way He ministers to us and sustains us in the natural; it is the way to prosperity and success. In the New Testament, we are admonished to *think on these things* (Philippians 4:8). God tells us what to think about and thinking on those things will promote and maintain the alpha wave pattern of brain activity.

Use **all** of your brain by letting God work through you. After the widow woman at Zarephath sustained the prophet, Elijah *first, so e*ven in a famine, God sustained her. When the man of God asked, she did not refuse him, and God did not refuse her meal and oil, so she and her son ate for the duration of the drought. Put God first in your physical, natural life by putting Him first in your thought life.

Give that 10% over to God, in faith.

The Mind

God asks for 10%. What can God make out of 10 percent? 100%. Wholeness. Only God can do that. What can you make out of 10%? Use your mind and find out. *Let this mind be in me, that is in Christ Jesus,* (Philippians 2:5).

Jesus used all of His mind.

The tithe is 10%, the same amount that man is said to use of his mind, 10%. Maybe that's why it's so difficult for the natural, unsaved man to give that 10%, because it's *all* he has. If he gave 10% of his mind to God, what will he have with which to think?

But this should be a different story for the saved, born again, Spirit-filled man. We should have the Mind of Christ. Surely you don't think Jesus used only 10% of His brain. Why would we want the mind of Christ if it's not working at 100%? If we're using 10% of our brains and Jesus was doing the same, why would we trade? I'm using enough of my brain to know that doesn't make sense.

Jesus uses **all** of His brain, all of His mind, all of Himself, not to exhaustion however since Jesus is infinite. How could Jesus have done all those things He did at 10%? The things of God are a mystery to the world. They see it not. Could be because they are not using the other 90% of their brain. Too bad. Those in the Kingdom of God would make full use of their minds.

God does not waste. Why would He give you that big head you have and all those brain cells in it if you weren't supposed to be using *all* of it? So, use your mind of Christ when it's time to use your mind.

Give means to share, but it also means to yield under pressure. Which one are you doing? Are you giving willingly, or you just giving under pressure or out of fear? God loves the cheerful giver, and He will bless those who are willing and obedient. Not those who have to be talked into *appearing* obedient.

Abraham gave a tenth of all that God had blessed him with. And where did he give it? To Melchizedek, the high priest. He did it in obedience, thankfulness, and love. He gave 10% of all to the high priest as God instructed. What does God expect us to give?

- Our heart.
- Our treasure.
- Our time.
- Our bodies as a living sacrifice.

… to get?

Why does God say give? It's not to get stuff. We give because it shows that we have a heart of flesh. It also works the spiritual laws of God and activates the principle of Sow and Reap. But that's not the main reason to give. Why did God give? Why does He give? Love--, He loves us. God does not give to get stuff from us. So, we know that's not why we should give. We should be making ourselves, with God's direction and help into little Jesuses. We should do what we hear the Father say and do. We should try to be like Him. Jesus did not heal, give gifts, and et cetera to get praise and acclaim. That's not it. He did it because of LOVE.

If we had to give in order to get into Heaven, how many would make it? So that's not it, either.

Many of us just give to get. What would we want to get from God? It depends on who we are and who He is to us. It depends on our relationship with the Father. What does the baby Christian want from God? Stuff for the physical body, material goods, and financial gifts. Asking God to pay your utility bill or any other financial gift is the same thing as asking Him for money.

Beloved. I wish above all things that thou mayest prosper and be in health, even as thy soul prospereth.

3 John 1:2

Come out of the flesh, move into the soul, and then into the spirit realm. You can't reach God in your flesh, but that's what we are almost always seeking Him for. It's really hard to think about your flesh when you're in the Spirit. We want our flesh protected, nurtured, guarded, and kept. Instead of asking God for flesh things, we should empty our vessel and ask God to fill it with *spiritual* things such as Wisdom, knowledge, Fruits of the Spirit, anointing for Kingdom work. Then we'd never have to worry about being refused when making requests of God.

We don't have to beg God to keep *His* anointing. So, if purpose and anointing are in you, He will automatically keep it. Our flesh must decrease so He can increase. If you don't refuse His Holy Spirit or His anointing, then God won't refuse you.

Remember that anointing is for ministry.

Bad Manners

If you are not paying 10%, if you are not tithing, it all boils down to bad manners. The tithe is 10% and if God says tithe and you're not, that disobedience is making *spiritual debt*. Tithing is the response to what you have already received from God. The tithe is what you pay God for what He has already given you. The tithe belongs to God.

When somebody hands you something, you say thank you. That's good manners. When God allows you to get, have, and be all that you are, got, and have, *Thank you*, should be easy to say. But God says that faith without works is dead, so you must not just say, *thank you*. You must **do** thank you. With God that *doing,* that action is **paying** the tithe.

Luke recounts the story of ten lepers who Jesus healed. They were cured of leprosy, then He told them to go and show themselves to the priest, and they did. Only one came back to thank Jesus. Only one. Jesus asked that man, **Weren't there nine others of you?** And the man replied that there were. Luke 17:19 reads: **And he said unto him, arise, and go thy way, thy faith hath made thee whole.**

Only one man out of 10 came back to say, *Thank you,* Jesus, to glorify God because of what He had done for him. That is what your tithe does. It glorifies God. The nine who in their times (or today) receive either financially, physically, or spiritually, who do not turn and glorify the Father, by actions and testimony are not made whole. The one who came back to thank Jesus was made whole. Nine were cleansed of leprosy but were not made *whole.*

What does that mean?

Just because ten men had leprosy does not mean that that was *all* that was wrong with them. They may have been remedied of one malady and granted, it was a humdinger, but what about the rest of their needs and brokenness? What about the restoration of the nine into society? Their finances, their general health, emotions and family? Because of coming back to say, *thank you* after being blessed one man was made whole.

The unsaved man isn't just *spiritually* corrupt, he has **symptoms** of spiritual corruption. But most often, his health (flesh) and soul are afflicted as well. Leprosy was a symptom of a soul affliction or a spiritual disorder, (sin). Even today most who come to God don't come because their spirit is not right. How easy it would be to witness and win souls if people could discern disorders in their spirits. Instead, they may not come until the soul or flesh manifests a problem. When it hurts physically, emotionally, or financially, when flesh becomes uncomfortable, when the world, can't fix it, heal it, make it go away, or make it stop hurting, man looks for God. He knows he must have Salvation in order to access healing, so he may accept Salvation for temporal reasons for the comfort of his flesh.

That's why so many get saved at big services, but you never see them again. They got what they wanted from God--, or so they think. No one can trick God.

Or they couldn't get what they wanted from God. Not really wanting God, just what He had.

What man needs is *wholeness*. The ones that come back into the House of God to say, *thank you*, week after week are the ones built up and restored to wholeness. Wholeness comes after the act of tithing. Your tithes are your *thank you* to God. Without it you're operating in bad manners, and you cannot be made whole. Jesus said, *"Your faith has made you whole."*

Without faith enough to pay your tithe, you cannot be made whole.

Because you don't pay your tithe, you might have a little more change in your pocket today than the guy who pays his tithe, but you might not.

Later in life when you are on your sick- or deathbed worrying about how your children will fight over all your money that you have earned and saved up all your life, and not enjoyed--, or when it's all said and done, you may be broke because of not tithing, no matter how much money you made. The faithful tither is healthy and enjoying his children, prosperity and life. His children are also prosperous, because of good manners.

I know your Mama taught you to say, *Thank you?* **Then tithe**.

Road Under Construction

We're marching up to Zion, the beautiful city of God. We're marching up the Kings Highway. No one can walk up there but the pure in heart...

Did you know that **the road to hell is** *paved*?

They say the road to hell is paved with many good intentions. The road to hell is both paved and broad, and that's a lot of work. Is that road broad because there are so many sinners, because so many are working on paving the road to hell as if they are in a chain gang? Is it paved because so many are chained in the bondage of sin? (The wages of sin is death, (Romans 8:23.) Is it paved because so many may have to use it? Pray not.

Where Does God Walk?

All of us want to walk with God, *right*? We are made in His image and likeness, and we shall be like Him. We want to be like Him. Many think we already are. But **can two you walk together except they agree?** (Amos 3:3)

If you want to walk with God, you need to know where He walks.

- Invite Him (prayer, praise, worship.)
- Make your place home, and person inviting.
- If you're going to walk with God, you've got to walk where He walks, on that which He walks.
    As God steps, all creation bows.

Many Are Called

All Creation recognizes its fullness of time when God is present. In order to serve Him, Creation matures, ripens, and becomes perfected. When God steps into the picture as Lord of the Harvest, all Creation knows that it is time for harvest; everything is designed to serve and honor the Lord, recognizing that **it *is* the fullness of time**.

The fig tree (Mark 11:21) got cursed because **Jesus** was passing by that tree. From afar off, it looked like a healthy tree that should have had fruit on it. Don't you see that was **Jesus** coming up to a tree that should have borne much fruit, yet there was none. That tree was either in rebellion or not properly connected so it could bear. Its sole purpose is to serve, especially the King of kings. **If it does not live in and for its purpose, then it has no purpose**; it must and will die. **Neither a tree nor a man can just *change* his purpose.** Reiterating, that was Jesus, anyone else may not have known the purpose of the fruit, the purpose of that creation, the purpose of everything created by God in Heaven and on Earth and below the Earth. But that was Jesus; and He certainly knew.

More than your boss at work when the one who knows your **purpose** shows up, you'd better be in it. You'd better be ready or getting ready. When you see Jesus, you should grow up. You should grow up some, every time you see Him--, from glory to glory, every time you meet Him, whether in prayer, praise, worship, meditation, or in the Word. You should mature or be reaching toward maturity in some way.

When Jesus comes up to you, will there be *fruit*?

All Creation serves Him, and if we serve Him, it serves the Christ in you.

That which is *under* the Earth serves you by getting rid of your enemies for you. How? We know the devil is always working against folks, and **that includes *your* enemies.** Your ungodly enemies are also enemies of God and they do not have God as a shield or help to fight their battles or to help them overcome the devil. Those who have made deals with the devil will either have to deal with the devil or be dealt with by the devil. A kingdom divided against itself will fall. We already know the kingdom that will fall is Satan's kingdom because we finished the Book. As the Devil's kingdom fights against itself, it takes out your enemies as well. Things under the Earth serve you. All of Creation is made to serve you. You should walk in that.

God says He spews out lukewarm water and, most likely, unripe fruit. As an apple tree bears 1000 apples for example, every apple is *called* forth from the seed that produced it, yet at harvest time only the **ripe** fruit is chosen, not the green fruit, not the over ripe, or the rotten fruit. The tree may not render 1000 good apples, and maybe only 500 or less when the Apple Picker comes to harvest. Only the fruit in its season is chosen. Many are *called*, but few are **chosen**. If you are in step with God, if you are acknowledging Him to direct your steps and maturing as He says you should, you will be in *your season* when He comes.

If you are trying to rush your ministry, your successes, favor and awards--, even your life, when your real season comes you will be over ripe, rotten and passed over. You may end up as mulch or fertilizer for the fruit that is in its *season*. Don't rush your ministry or your life!

Only the devil picks immature fruit. God is not interested in unripe, overruns, or imperfects. The Lord deserves the best; and it is with our best that we serve Him. That is what He was teaching Cain in the Book of Genesis. Doing it any way but God's way leads to debt creation.

Flesh creation leads to debt creation.

If a dignitary came to your town, people would want to serve him. Many wouldn't even charge money. They just want the honor of saying So-and-So was here. How much more for God? All creation has sense enough to know the honor and the purpose is to serve Him.

Don't procrastinate in your spiritual growth, especially your soul's prosperity. In due season, you do not want to be passed over.

On What does God Walk?

Red carpet, rose petals, what? Two can walk together only if they are in agreement. Don't expect God to walk on what *you* walk on. You have to make *your* walk line up with what **He** walks on. Let's see, God lives in Heaven. There are Gates about the City with a Pearl on each. The streets are paved with gold. The saints in Heaven tread on gold.

In Heaven they worship God and walk on gold, not the other way around.

Either gold is not very valuable in Heaven because everything else up there is more valuable, or maybe they are not any better things to walk on.. Perhaps there's so much gold there that they can't think of anything else to do with it. Or our God is just *all that*. I prefer to say that God is ***all that*** even though the other choices are good, He can just walk on what we feel is so precious on Earth.

God, the Angels and the Saints of God are so precious that gold is waiting to serve them.

God is telling us something: *He is <u>all that</u>.*

When you walk on something, the placement of it under your feet tells you something about its importance or lack of value. Its priority is identified by who it serves and *how* it serves. It can especially tell you about the importance of **what** or **who** is standing on this thing of value.

God has placed tremendous value on His saints in Heaven to allow them to also walk on gold. God's will should be done on Earth as it is in Heaven. We are also His saints, and we can walk on gold too. As we do, we agree with Him. As we walk correctly, He will walk with us. Now as we walk, we talk. *He walks with me, and He talks with me, and He tells me I am His own.* Do you know that beautiful hymn? If you are walking and talking with someone, you have their ear, you have audience, you have *relationship*. Hopefully it's a deep and permanent relationship. Now you can tell Him how you're doing, and what you're doing. Since you are wise enough to know that He is wiser, you won't talk too much, but will **listen**. He can advise you, counsel and guide you. As He came down to talk with Adam in the Garden, they too walked and talked together.

Enoch walked with God; they were in agreement (Genesis 5:24).

Where will you walk? Where does the road lead? Where does it go? That's where you walk. That road should go towards your goals, purpose and destiny, into your future.

As long as you are living, moving, breathing, having your being and growing in spiritual matters, your road is always under construction. God has established your path, your comings and goings, but you must be in *agreement* with Him to walk with Him.

If you kept following yesterday's path, you could be off the road today. If you stay on today's path, you might be off the road for tomorrow if you follow tomorrow's path and you may miss Eternity. God changes not, but the road is always ***under construction*** because of *your* will, *your* choices, and *your* actions. Why all these intersections and seeming path changes? God wants to know that you are listening, that you are listening, and that you are listening. Life is dynamic. Things around you are changing constantly. Your changes in path and direction are related to the nature of the spiritual world you live in. It is related to spiritual warfare, and you must strategically be on the offensive and defend the spiritual ground that on which God has placed you. You must listen to God's voice 24/7. He wants to know that you are listening and obeying. Faith comes by hear***ing***, and that's progressive. God is progressive. Faith comes by hear*ing*.

Saying or thinking, *I've already heard that* is not faith. Knowledge comes by having heard. Faith comes by hearing. That's progressive. Not once and not one time only.

Paved

„„And they saw God of Israel. And there were under his feet, as it were a work of sapphire stone. And as it were, the body of heaven in his clearness. (Exodus 24:10)

Gold is enduring, it wears gracefully. The heavenly streets are no doubt perfect. They are shiny, not pitted, dented or scratched. They are perfect and real--, and not made of the Wizard of Oz's counterfeit yellow bricks.

The road to hell is probably paved with asphalt, the same stuff with which the world has paved millions of miles of Earth roads. Did you know you can only pour asphalt when the outside temperatures are very high? That's why crews work in sweltering heat to pave roads. There are some other crews in a hellish fury covered with sin sweat paving, hell bound roads. Those have sin, curses, debt, and iniquity in their bloodline and just can't help themselves.

No wonder so many Christians are falling down potholes, manholes, sinkholes, or running off the path because of *soft shoulders*. Come on, Church. We need to be witnessing to those souls and snatching them from the path of sin and death.

And Christians are not supposed to be getting used to asphalt. We're supposed to be getting used to **gold**. Laying down the gold neither means rejecting wealth nor embracing poverty. Not at all. Jesus is walking on gold, but He is surrounded by riches and glory. I want to agree with that in Earth so I can walk with Him—on gold. And so can you.

The road to hell is paved. What about the road to Heaven? The King's highway? The devil can't have a better road than we do. If he does no wonder people keep choosing it. Especially if you are fond of your car, you won't drive it down the road with potholes and loose gravel if a smooth ride on a well-paved road is available. **Be diligent to know where all paved roads are going**. Folks covered with sins are still paving those hell bound roads.

Don't refuse me, Lord; Lord, help my debt. God will not refuse an inviting invitation on a road of agreement. Lay down the gold, put God first and walk on the gold. Don't hoard it, God says, **Show Me, you're not afraid. Walk**

where I walk. Walk where I say walk and walk and what I walk on.

As we walk and talk, you can tell God of your needs. As you walk in your purpose and toward your destiny, God has commanded blessings along your way, even cancellation and mitigation of physical *and* spiritual debt. The Lord will help you get out of debt. Get on the right path to be where God will walk with you and you can walk with God. Be where the blessings are waiting for you, because the answers to your prayers are always Yes, and Amen!

Jubilee

The year of jubilee (Leviticus 25:9). Some Bible scholars argue on what that Jubilee actually was. Some say it was not the cancellation of all financial debt but the termination of certain leases where a person of wealth used a lesser man's land to pay off a debt the poorer man owed.

I know we serve a debt canceling God who loves us and will redeem us fully from every curse of the Law, in Jesus Christ. May the Lord grant Jubilee to you, your life, your family – your entire bloodline. Amen.

Jesus taught us to pray this way: Forgive us our debts as we forgive others. In Bible times, every seventh year, debts were forgiven.

May you have a seventh year Jubilee in the Lord right now in the Name of Jesus.

Rest in the LORD. If God can save your soul and He can save your life from the torments and losses of spiritual debt, then He will do that or even more for financial debt. He is a debt-canceling, soul prospering God, giving blessings that make rich and add no sorrow. May the Lord bless you richly and add no sorrow with it, Amen.

There's reason to sound the trumpet there and rejoice! The LORD has relieved, alleviated, canceled or retired debt for many in the Bible. There is precedence: May the LORD cancel all debt in your life, spiritual and natural, in the Name of Jesus, Amen.

Thank you for purchasing this volume, we pray for your complete victory over spiritual and financial debt, lack, insufficiency, and, or poverty in the name of Jesus.

Amen.

Enjoy Bible teaching and messages on the Dr. Miles YouTube Channel. Find spiritual warfare prayers on the Warfare Prayer Channel on YouTube.

Christian books by this author

AK: Adventures of the Agape Kid

AMONG SOME THIEVES

As My Soul Prospers

Behave

Churchzilla (The Wanna-Be Bride of Christ)

The Coco-So-So Correct Show

Demons Hate Questions

Devil Weapons: *Anger, Unforgiveness & Bitterness*

Do Not Orphan Your Seed

Do Not Work for Money

Don't Refuse Me Lord

The FAT Demons

got Money?

Let Me Have a Dollar's Worth

Living for the NOW of God

Lord, Help My Debt

Lose My Location

Made Perfect In Love

The Man Safari *(Really, I'm Just Looking)*

Marriage Ed., *Rules of Engagement & Marriage*

The Motherboard: *Key to Soul Prosperity*

Name Your Seed

Plantation Souls

The Poor Attitudes of Money

Power Money: Nine Times the Tithe

The Power of Wealth

Seasons of Grief

Seasons of War

SOULS in Captivity

Soul Prosperity: Your Health & Your Wealth

The *spirit* of Poverty

The Throne of Grace, *Courtroom Prayers*

Time Is of the Essence

Triangular Powers (4 book series)

Warfare Prayer Against Poverty

When the Devourer is Rebuked

The Wilderness Romance

Other Journals & Devotionals by this author:

The Cool of the Day – ***Journal***

got HEALING? Verses for Life

got HOPE? Verses for Life

got GRACE? Verses for Life

got JOY? Verses for Life

got PEACE? Verses for Life

got LOVE? Verses for Life

He Hears Us, Prayer Journal *4 colors*

I Have A Star, Dream Journal *kids, teen, adult*

I Have A Star, Guided Prayer Journal**,**

J'ai une Etoile, Journal des Reves

Let Her Dream, Dream Journal

Men Shall Dream, Dream Journal,

My Favorite Prayers (in 4 styles)

My Sowing Journal (in three different colors)

Tengo una Estrella, Diario de Sueños

<u>Illustrated children's books by this author:</u>

Big Dog (8-book series)

Do Not Say That to Me

Every Apple

Fluff the Clouds

I Love You All Over the World

Imma Dance

The Jump Rope

Kiss the Sun

www.ingramcontent.com/pod-product-compliance
Lightning Source LLC
LaVergne TN
LVHW051419080426
835508LV00022B/3164